For my mother, Okleki.

— Samuel

I dedicate this book to my mother, Jackie.
She made me the person I am today.

— Freda

I dedicate this book to all the children out
there who miss their parents.

— Alisa

CHASING
A SPIDER

Chasing A Spider Publishing (Columbus and Sacramento)

Text copyright © 2021 by Samuel Narh and Freda Narh

Illustration copyright © 2021 by Alisa Knatko

Published by Chasing A Spider Publishing

Text edited by Jennifer Rees

Book design by David Miles

LCCN: 2021922159

ISBN: 9781734789720

First Edition

Printed in China

10 9 8 7 6 5 4 3 2 1

Milko

SAMUEL NARH
FREDA NARH
and
ILLUSTRATED BY
ALISA KNATKO

Milko misses Mama like leaves
long for the rain this dry season.

In the glow of the morning sun, Abena, his younger sister, cries endlessly.

For what? Milko doesn't think Papa knows.

Perhaps, he's never going to figure that out now.

The porridge is boiling over, and the cat is after the dog.

Milko reaches for his
mirror behind the couch.
He feels older now.
His voice comes from a
warm place.

He wonders why Abena
cries so much.
Where does her shrill
voice come from?
Papa can't console her.

Just then, another
question soars
across his mind like
a wild dove from
the East.
When is Mama
coming back?

Her embrace is as tender as a petal.
The aroma of her delicious foods lingers on.
"Milko, listen!" is her constant refrain.
Her smile consoles him.

In his mirror, Milko sees Papa getting ready for the market.

Unlike Mama, Papa is terrible at haggling with the fishmongers. He drifts through the market, and he always forgets something.

Milko dislikes how the old shopkeepers
rub his hair and play with his cheeks.
He likes going to the market with Mama.
She buys him *salteñas*.

How long is a year?
Papa says a year is 365 days, most of the times.
Mama's journey to Ethiopia seems longer than
a year to Milko.

She's been
gone since the
beginning of the
rainy season.
Why is Mama at
the horn of Africa,
so far away from
Bolivia?

Night falls in
Ethiopia first,
but Milko knows
that his days are
longer here.

He counts his days
in tens on a wall.
The rainy season
is here again, and
the leaves smile
endlessly. Yet, Milko
still doesn't have
Mama's warm
embrace.

Abena cries when Mama
calls from the East.
Oh Abena, where does your
shrill voice come from?
Maybe, it's a longing for
the gleam in Mama's eyes.

Milko can see that those tears make Papa miss Mama. It also makes Milko yearn for the rewards he gets for not chasing both the cat and the dog.

Milko marks 365 days on his wall, and Mama isn't here. He sleeps with the mirror in his hand to watch those secret tears roll down his cheeks.

Milko hears a familiar voice in his sleep.
A laughter as deep as the forest slips into his room.

Someone plugs a kiss on his cheek.
Milko sees Mama's soft face.

In a hazy bliss, he staggers to add another day on his wall, for it's a Leap Year.